Copier Creations

Also by Paul Fleischman

Picture Books
Time Train
Shadow Play
Rondo in C
The Birthday Tree

Novels
Bull Run
Townsend's Warbler
The Borning Room
Saturnalia
Rear-View Mirrors
Path of the Pale Horse
The Half-A-Moon Inn

Short Story Collections
Coming-and-Going Men: Four Tales
Graven Images: Three Stories

Poetry
Joyful Noise: Poems for Two Voices
I Am Phoenix: Poems for Two Voices